Beyond
the Call
of Duty

KT-215-818

PERSONAL BRAVERY
IN WARTIME

C333675909

Published in paperback in 2015 by Wayland
Copyright © Wayland 2015

Wayland
338 Euston Road
London NW1 3BH

Wayland Australia
Level 17/207 Kent Street
Sydney, NSW 2000

Editor: Annabel Stones
Designer: Elaine Wilkinson
Author and main researcher: Peter Hicks
Researchers: Hester Vaizey, Laura Simpson and Edward Field
at The National Archives

The National Archives looks after the UK government's historical documents. It holds records dating back nearly 1,000 years from the time of William the Conqueror's Domesday Book to the present day. All sorts of documents are stored there, including letters, photographs, maps and posters. They include great Kings and Queens, famous rebels like Guy Fawkes and the strange and unusual – such as reports of UFOs and even a mummified rat!

Material reproduced courtesy of The National Archives,
London, England.
www.nationalarchives.gov.uk

Catalogue references and picture acknowledgements (Images from The National Archives unless otherwise stated): Cover (top left) & p.15 (top left): ZPER 34/147 f425 Carrier pigeons on active service with the French Army using a converted bus, 1915; Cover (bottom left) & p.11 (bottom): RAIL 253/516 (6) Trooper 'Gunner' Wilcox & horse; Cover (centre medal) & p.4 (top): PDSA: The PDSA Dickin Medal; Cover (bottom right) & p.8: AIR 4/58 Photograph of airman with dog from the logbook of Squadron Leader B J E Lane, Battle of Britain pilot 1940; p.1 & p.5 (bottom): AIR 4/58 Photograph from the logbook of Squadron Leader B J E Lane, Battle of Britain pilot 1940; p.2 & p.17 (main): INF 2/44/191 Carrier pigeons 1944–1945; p.4 (bottom): Sergeant Alison Baskerville RLC/MoD/Crown Copyright; p.5 (top): Peter Hicks; p.6, p.10, p.18, p.20 & p.30 (bottom): Shutterstock (poppies); p.7 (top): Popperfoto/Getty Images; p.7 (bottom): IWM via Getty Images; p.8 (top): WO 188/911 War dog wearing a respirator 1943–1944; p.9: INF3-713 Ditty Box Dog attacking parachutist Artist Spurrier; p.11 (top): IWM via Getty Images; p.12: COPY 1/209 (31) Hunting scene 1903; p.13 (top): INF 2/44 London after the Blitz, Old Bailey and Figure of Justice from Ludgate Hill 1944–1945; p.13 (bottom): AIR 40/2541(e) V2 transporter and associated equipment 1945; p.14: WO 208/3508 (2) War pigeon illustration 1917–1918; p.15 (right): WO 208/3508 (1) War pigeons 1917–1918; p.16: WO 208/3565 Peacetime organisation of Pigeon Service Note to finder of pigeon 1944–1945; p.17 (top): KV 4/10 Press cutting, use of carrier pigeons in War work 1945–1951; p.19 (top): Mondadori via Getty Images; p.19 (bottom): Shutterstock; p.21 (top): INF 3/1690 Indian troops loading mule cart; p.21 (bottom): Shutterstock; p.22: CO 1069/730 A Camel caravan bringing shingle for construction work 1908–1934; p.23 (top): MPI 1/720/1 Middle East peace map presented to cabinet by T E Lawrence, 1918; p.23 (centre): COPY 1/514/560 (a) Elephant At Work, Burma, 1907; p.24 & p.25 (top): THE POLISH INSTITUTE AND SIKORSKI MUSEUM – LONDON; p.25 (bottom): FO 898/527 German troops occupy Poland 1939; p.26: INF 3/764b Ditty Box Cat with sailors on messdeck Artist Victor J Bertoglio; p.27 (top): INF 3/764a Ditty Box Cat with sailors on messdeck Artist Victor J Bertoglio; p.27 (bottom): The Regimental Museum of the Royal Welsh, Brecon; p.28: KV 4/10 (2) Sack for release of Carrier Pigeons; p.29 (top left): INF 3/1026 Girl, boy and pigeon Artist Betty Swanwick; p.29 (top right): E 36/274 (112) Littere Wallie, marginalia drawing of horseman with spear c1282–1292; p.29 (bottom): 800px A researcher working with delicate resource at The National Archives.
Background images and other graphic elements courtesy of Shutterstock.

Disclaimer: Every effort has been made to trace the copyright holder but if you feel you have the rights to any images contained in this book then please contact the publisher.
Please note:
The website addresses (URLs) included in this book were valid at the time of going to press. However, because of the nature of the Internet, it is possible that some addresses may have changed, or sites may have changed or closed down since publication. While the author and publishers regret any inconvenience this may cause to the readers, no responsibility for any such changes can be accepted by either the author or the publishers.

A cataloguing record for this title is available at the British Library.

ISBN 978 0 7502 8415 8

Dewey Number 355.4'24'0929

Printed in China

10 9 8 7 6 5 4 3 2 1

Wayland is a division of Hachette Children's Books, an Hachette UK company
www.hachette.co.uk

CONTENTS

ANIMALS IN WAR

For thousands of years mankind has used animals in warfare. The Ancient Egyptians used horses to pull their light and mobile chariots. The Assyrians and Arabs trained horses and camels for their cavalry charges. Enemies of Rome took elephants into their battles against the early Roman Army. Animals also played a vital role in the two World Wars.

Although much is made of human bravery in warfare, the role of animals has been neglected. They too have performed extraordinary feats of courage on behalf of humans but have been largely forgotten in history. It was not until 1943 that their efforts were officially recognised. In that year, the People's Dispensary for Sick Animals awarded its PDSA Dickin Medal for animal bravery in conflict.

◀ The PDSA Dickin Medal.

Named after Maria Dickin, the founder of the PDSA, the large bronze medal is inscribed with the words 'For Gallantry – We Also Serve'. The ribbon is coloured green, dark brown and pale blue, representing the water, earth and air of the Navy, Army and Air Force.

◀ The tradition of goat mascots in the British Army dates from the 18th century.

▲ Mules carrying ammunition and a field gun at the Animals in War Memorial, London.

The huge suffering and contribution of animals in warfare has recently been recognised. In 2004 a memorial was unveiled on Park Lane in London to the millions of animals who have died 'in the cause of human freedom'. The curved stone wall is covered in carvings and inscriptions, and there are bronze sculptures of a war horse, two mules and a dog. The memorial bears a very truthful statement about animals in war: 'THEY HAD NO CHOICE'.

'This monument is dedicated to all the animals that served and died alongside the British and Allied forces in wars and campaigns throughout time.'

This is the dedication on the Animals in War Memorial, London.

Animals at War

Both World Wars are often thought to have been mechanised conflicts, but in fact, animals were a lifeline on all fronts. Because of geography and local conditions, front-line troops would not have been able to do their jobs without the assistance of animals; as haulers and carriers of equipment, messengers, bomb detectors, search and rescue experts, protectors and loyal companions.

A dog provides company for a group of Battle of Britain pilots in 1940.

DOG TRAINING SCHOOL

Compared to the other European powers in World War I, Britain was slow to see the value of dogs in warfare. When the war broke out in August 1914, Germany had 6,000 dogs ready to go into service, whereas Britain only had one! It was not until 1916 that Lieutenant Colonel E.H. Richardson was given permission to start a messenger dog training school.

Lines of communication at the front were very important but they were often broken or damaged. When a message had to be sent dogs were faster and less of a target than trench runners.

Training dogs for the Western Front needed to be tough. It was important to get them used to explosions. They were only fed once a day and just before feeding, hand grenades were deliberately exploded. The food was taken away after the last explosion, so if the dogs had been too timid they went hungry. The more hungry they became, the less scared they were. Richardson knew that dogs who ate at the first explosion would do well in the front line. It was found that Airedales, collies and whippets made excellent messenger dogs, and dogs with dark coats were preferred because they were more difficult to spot.

Dogs were used for other tasks, too. They guarded stores and ration dumps, carried ammunition to front-line troops, ran telephone wires between trenches and made excellent sentries. Enemy raiding parties often attacked trenches at night to try and capture soldiers for questioning. An alert guard dog was very useful in discouraging them.

One of the most useful tasks dogs performed was ratting. Conditions around the lines were often filthy and unheathy which led to

▲ Injured dogs in the Austrian Army being transported to the animal hospital by dog ambulance!

a huge rat population. Soldiers hated rats so dogs were used to keep the population down. One officer bragged that his adopted dog, a large French foxhound, could kill up to 27 rats – 'the size of rabbits' – a day!

A SECOND THOUGHT
The training of dogs to prepare them for the trenches seems cruel. Why was it so tough?

Trench Warfare

By the end of 1914 on the Western Front, both sides had dug in and created a network of trenches that stretched from the North Sea to the Swiss border. Why were soldiers fighting in this way? Rapid-firing machine guns and heavy artillery made it essential for soldiers to be out of the line of fire and have shelter below ground. There were three lines of trenches: fire, support and reserve. Getting messages to headquarters could be very difficult, so messenger dogs were important.

▲ A messenger dog on the Western Front, 1918. A Sergeant inserts a message into the special cylinder attached to the collar.

PATROLS AND PARACHUTES

By World War II the ability of dogs to help the war effort had been recognised. It was also during this war that the People's Dispensary for Sick Animals introduced the Dickin Medal – a Victoria Cross for animals.

Name:
Ricky (Welsh Collie)

Event: Mine clearing, after World War II

Location:
Nederweent, Holland

Medal:
PDSA Dickin Medal

Date Awarded:
29 March 1947

One strength dogs have is the ability to smell danger. Bob, a collie dog, was part of a platoon on a night patrol in North Africa in 1943. With his white patches painted over, he led the patrol behind enemy lines but, suddenly, he refused to move.

Wondering what the problem was, a couple of men went ahead. About 200 metres away was the enemy. If Bob had not stopped, the patrol would have been ambushed.

▼ **A Flight Sergeant pets an Alsatian dog at a fighter station during the Battle of Britain in 1940.**

Incredibly, some dogs were trained to parachute and were dropped into war zones in North Africa, Italy and northern France. Rob, the 'para-dog', was a veteran of 20 jumps and knew the procedure well. When he landed, he lay totally still and silent until his handler unclipped the parachute.

One of the many problems troops faced after D-Day landings in Normandy were mines. These hidden bombs detonated when a person or vehicle applied pressure to them. The sniffer dogs that were used on D-Day were invaluable. They would search for mines and when they found one would sit dead still. Just after the war, a Welsh collie named Ricky was clearing a canal bank of mines at Nederweent in Holland, when one exploded, killing a soldier. Ricky was injured in the head, but remained calm and carried on seeking out more mines.

An Alsatian called Irma did remarkable work during the second Blitz (1944–45), when the V1 and V2 bombs were falling on London. She had the most amazing sense of smell and helped the Civil Defence to locate victims buried in the ruins of bombed buildings. When she found a victim, she would sit quite still and the workers would start digging carefully. Irma found 191 people, 21 of whom were still alive.

All of these dogs were awarded the Dickin Medal for their bravery.

A SECOND THOUGHT
What special equipment would a dog need to work with front-line troops?

▲ Dogs were excellent for guarding high-security military bases and installations.

D-Day Dog

Bing, another Alsatian, was parachuted into Normandy during the D-Day landings on 6 June 1944. Although injured after becoming trapped in a tree, he played a vital part in his company's advance into German-occupied France. D-Day was important because it trapped the German forces between the Red Army in the east and British and American troops in the west. This meant Germany could not win the war. Once the Allied troops got a foothold on the coast, they pushed deep into France and by 25 August Paris was liberated.

HORSES AT THE FRONT

The use of horses in traditional cavalry charges was rare on the Western Front (1914-18) because of murderous machine-gun fire, but horses were immensely useful in other ways. However, trench warfare was not kind to horses and the poor conditions pushed them to the limits of misery.

When war broke out, there was a serious shortage of horses in the British Army. As well as importing thousands from abroad, many privately owned horses were conscripted into the Army. After tearful appeals from children, it was decided that horses under 15 hands would not be used.

Early in the war, the British Expeditionary Force (BEF) were forced to retreat from Mons, Belguim. Horses gallantly assisted men to safety, but many were driven to exhaustion. Because saddles were kept on for so long, their backs became very sore and the stone roads were hard on their legs. Many horses were so tired they fell asleep at their artillery harness poles, grazing their knees as they slumped forward.

As the war of movement gave way to static trench warfare, horses were used to move heavy supplies – such as rations and ammunition – up to the front line. This meant they were vulnerable to artillery shelling and many received shrapnel wounds. When a shell exploded hot lead and metal flew in all directions and horses, being tall, often got hit.

It was the weather and conditions that caused major problems. France and Belgium have very wet and cold winters and when the rain fell, the areas behind and in the trenches became soft and boggy, often trapping horses, wagons and men. The bitter cold was cruel to horses as most were not used to nights in the open.

Poison gas was first used in World War I and precautions had to be taken.

So Much Mud!

The war was fought on farmland and in the heavy rain the churned-up earth turned to liquid mud. To make matters worse, the Germans took the higher ground in 1914, leaving the British defending valleys into which all the water drained. Shell holes were a hazard and if horses slipped into them, it was impossible to get them out. Men witnessed trapped horses barely visible in a sea of mud.

▲ Pack horse carrying rubber trench boots through a sea of mud. The Somme, 1916.

At first pinning plugs into horses' nostrils was tried, but this was too painful. Gas masks, similar to nose-bags, were then introduced. Gas casualties were relatively low – out of 2,000 cases, 211 died.

If it had not been for the Army Veterinary Corps, the situation for injured horses would have been far worse. They were helped by RSPCA inspectors who had a deep knowledge of horses. Their hospitals treated over a million wounded and sick horses throughout the war.

A SECOND THOUGHT

How do you think the troops felt when the animals they were in charge of suffered in the war?

▼ In the last weeks of World War I, when the fighting was on open country, the cavalry was much more useful.

A LUCKY CHARM

By the time of World War II (1939–45), the British had adopted the idea of mechanised warfare. They didn't think that tanks, lorries or troop carriers would break down. The Germans, however, had seen how motorised transport broke down in the Spanish Civil War (1936–39), so that when the war started they had over 100,000 horses ready.

Name:
Olga and Upstart

Date: 1944

Event: The Blitz

Location: London

Medal:
PDSA Dickin Medal

Date Awarded:
11 April 1947

Not surprisingly, the War Office immediately decided that 9,000 horses were needed for use in Palestine in the Middle East. The Army bought most of the horses from local fox hunts, but the journey over land and sea in a freezing winter was a nightmare for men and horses. Nearly 1,000 were badly injured or died.

The 8,000 survivors made up the First Cavalry Division and proved effective in keeping the front quiet.

British forces fighting deep behind Japanese lines in Burma in 1944 had an unexpected arrival in the middle of battle. One of the pack-ponies suddenly went into labour and amongst the exploding mortar bombs a tiny foal was born. The battle-hardened Chindits melted as news of this miraculous birth spread through the 77th Brigade. Too young and small to be a pack-horse like her mother, 'Minnie' became a lucky charm for the men. She survived a number of battles and injuries. Against all the rules, she was flown out of the Burmese rainforest to the Lancashire Fusilier's base in India and became their mascot!

◀ Local fox hunts were a good source of horses for the Army during 1939–40.

▲ The 'Blitzed' streets of London in which police horses had to work.

Back in Britain, horses were helping in the Blitz. Olga was on patrol in 1944 when a bomb exploded right next to her. After being startled, she returned to her job of helping the injured and crowd control. Upstart was on patrol in Bethnal Green when a bomb exploded 20 metres away, covering her with glass and debris. However, she carried on directing the traffic and helping the crowds.

A SECOND THOUGHT
How do you think the owners felt when they had to sell their horses to the Army? Would they be worried?

The Blitz

The Blitz was the bombing of major towns and cities by the Luftwaffe during 1940–41. At one point, London was bombed for 57 consecutive nights. Police horses were well suited to air raids, because their training involved crowd noise and gun shots, although exploding bombs and anti-aircraft fire were much noisier. There was a second Blitz during 1944–45 when V weapons started falling on London and the south-east. Over 500 V2s hit London causing huge damage and killing 2,700 civilians.

▲ A V2 rocket. The world's first ballistic missile sped towards its target at 4,800 kilometres per hour.

SMALL BIRD, BIG HEART

In the trenches during World War I it was easy for communications to break down. Homing and racing pigeons were fairly reliable ways of getting important messages to Headquarters from front-line trenches. They were even carried in tanks and aeroplanes for emergencies. Pigeons were capable of incredible feats of endurance and heroism.

The advantage of pigeons was that they had greater range than dogs, who could only manage about 8 kilometres. Lofts were built for them behind the lines and sometimes buses were converted into mobile coops. Each platoon was given two birds. On each pigeon's leg was a small aluminium tube into which an officer would insert a message written on paper. The bird was then released and flew back to the loft with the message.

There were some conditions in which pigeons did not fly well. If it was dark, raining or foggy it was difficult to persuade them to fly. There are stories of soaking wet pigeons who could not fly and on one occasion a soggy bird started walking towards the German lines with the message!

▲ Drawing showing how pigeons carried their important messages.

Pigeons were very brave. The French recognised this and awarded the Croix de Guerre and Croix Militaire to their heroic pigeons. The last pigeon sent from the besieged fortress of Verdun was badly injured flying through shell fire and shrapnel. He arrived at the loft but died as he delivered the message and was awarded the highest French decoration, the Légion d'Honneur. Decorated birds had specially painted message tubes on their legs.

▲ The French Army converted buses as mobile pigeon lofts.

Pigeon success rates were high. Of the 4,000 used during the Battle of the Somme, only 2 per cent failed to make it home. Overall, about 100,000 pigeons were used by the British armed forces, with a 95 per cent success rate of message delivery. They were fast too. When a seaplane ditched in the sea early in 1918, they sent a pigeon for help and it covered 35 kilometres (or 22 miles) in 22 minutes!

A SECOND THOUGHT

Soldiers in the front-line trenches were told they could not feed pigeons before sending messages. Why was this?

▲ For soldiers in difficult and dangerous positions, the success of a carrier pigeon could be a matter of life or death.

Send a Runner

Communication in the trenches was very important, but often very difficult. Telephone lines were always being damaged by artillery explosions, so dogs and pigeons were used as a back up. Pigeons were faster than dogs, but things did go wrong. One signaller remembers an officer asking for artillery support when his trench was attacked. The telephones were down, so they tried the pigeons, but neither would fly in the morning mist. They tried the dog, but it was was petrified by the noise and would not move. The officer surveyed the scene; 'Send a runner!' he ordered.

SPECIAL AGENT PIGEON

Despite the developments in technology of the inter-war years – the wireless and radar – pigeons still had a role to play in World War II. From helping crashed bomber crews to the Resistance movement in Europe, pigeons could communicate vital information and save lives.

Name:
William of Orange

Date:
September 1944

Event:
Arnhem Landings

Location:
Arnhem, Holland

Medal: PDSA Dickin Medal

Date Awarded: May 1945

All operational Resistance units in occupied Europe had a wireless operator. However, the Gestapo invested a lot of effort into trying to find and arrest these vital agents, so pigeons were used as back up. They would either be parachuted in containers for the Resistance to find or taken in by individual agents. Vital messages could be sent back as there were pigeon lofts all over the south-east of England. For example, Hen NPS 42.42004 was released in France with a message on 31 August 1944 at 2 pm. It reached Gillingham in Kent on 1 September at 2.25 pm, having flown 338 kilometres.

Pigeons could cover huge distances. There are examples of birds dropped deep into Germany that flew over 480 kilometres home in 48 hours. Pigeon William of

To Finder :—

If at sea, transmit by W/T for retransmission to Air Ministry.

If in Great Britain ; to nearest police or R.A.F. Station for retransmission ; or telephone ABBEY 3411 (forward charge) and ask for Signals Duty Officer.

Give FULL particulars in message, e.g.

"S.O.S. Colour: yellow in orange ; Aircraft No. M. 6199 ; 23/2/40 ; 1345 hours ; Position : 55°–14′N. 2°–21′E. In rubber dinghy."

It may be that the time, position and further detail is not filled in ; the message giving colour code, aircraft number and date, is not less important on that account.

Do not delay ! Do not lose the container.

(4775) Wt. 8421—109 40,000 4/40 T.S. 700
(5509—4778) Wt. 23418—1841 40,000 8/40 T.S. 700

▲ **Important instructions to finders of carrier pigeons, 1944.**

Orange flew 418 kilometres from Arnhem in Holland to Knutsford (217 kilometres over open sea) in 4 hours and 25 minutes.

In February 1942 a Beaufort Bomber crash landed in the icy water of the North Sea. The crew had one chance. The plane

A Helping Hand

The Resistance movement in Nazi-occupied Europe was a constant irritant to the German forces. The Special Operations Executive (SOE) in London sent in agents to help them and take part in important acts of sabotage. In France there were about twelve resistance groups with code-names such as, 'Jockey', 'Donkeyman' and 'Farmer'. They helped slow down the German response to the D-Day invasion by blowing up railway tracks, trains, bridges and roads. Pigeons carried messages of their work and successes.

▲ Altogether, 200,000 pigeons were given to the armed forces by their owners during World War II.

carried a chequered hen pigeon, Winkie, in a container. They found her and she flew off for RAF Leuchars. Sergeant Davidson found the exhausted oily bird and within 15 minutes the crew had been located and rescued. Winkie was the first ever recipient of the Dickin Medal.

In the battle for Italy in 1943, the 5th Infantry division made a request for air support to bomb a village being defended stubbornly by the Germans. Just as the bombers were ready to go, pigeon 'G.I. Joe' flew in with a message that the British 169th Brigade had just taken the village. If Joe had not flown his 32 kilometres in 20 minutes, at least 100 Allied lives would have been lost.

A SECOND THOUGHT

How do you think the Germans tried to stop pigeons returning to Britain with important messages?

◀ Between 1942 and 1945, over 16,000 pigeons were parachuted into Nazi-occupied countries.

THE OTHER WAR HORSES

Mules are the offspring of male donkeys and female horses. They were used successfully by the Indian Army in the 19th century. Tough, sturdy and stubborn, they were excellent pack animals in the mountains. By the time the British Army realised their value, World War I had broken out, so hundreds of thousands had to be imported from America.

The Army had recognised the mules' incredible stamina in the awful conditions of the Western Front, where they were able to carry vast quantities of equipment to and from the front line. Dozens of mules, tethered together in long lines, carried food, water, guns and ammunition to the men who needed it. Because they were so steady, they made excellent ammunition carriers. Special double panniers were made for them into which eight artillery shells were slotted. Each pair of mules had a driver who looked after them and these men had nothing but praise for the bravery and perseverance of their charges.

Dunny the mule was loved and revered by the men because he had been in the line since 1914. He was a survivor. He carried his loads at all hours in all weathers, even under fire, for two long years. No matter what the men did to him – they dressed him up in trousers, put old hats on him, twisted his tail – he just smiled. There was shrapnel in his hide, he had swollen knees, but every driver knew his special smile.

Feeding the mules (and horses) was extremely difficult. They were supposed to have nine kilograms of grain a day, but it rarely happened. They were always hungry and, being mules, they would eat anything – blankets, leather, even soldiers' uniforms. In the savagely cold winter of 1916–17, when the grain ran short, mules were fed sawdust cake! Water was constantly in short supply, but interestingly, neither horses nor mules ever drank the stagnant water from the shell holes.

▲ A mule carrying equipment for French troops on a mountain path during World War I.

As 1917 dragged on, the weather did not improve. The biggest killer was debility, which really meant exposure. In April, 26,319 mules were hospitalised because of intense cold. Many battle-hardened men broke down when they lost their animals.

A SECOND THOUGHT
Why do you think the drivers loved their mules so much?

Buying Mules

The story of how over 200,000 mules were bought by the British Army is a good insight into the huge organisation the war required. A mule was incredibly expensive, each costing £36, which was the equivalent of a private soldier's pay for two years! Most came from the Guyton and Harrington Mule Company in Lathrop, Missouri, USA – the 'mule capital of the world'. Rail links took them to Newport News, Virginia, where they were shipped to Britain.

▶ Mules are still used to help carry heavy loads today.

GALLANTRY ON ALL FRONTS

As mules had performed so well during World War I, when World War II broke out, the Army were very keen to use them again. 2,700 mules were shipped from Bombay to Marseilles and then taken to the French-Belgian border. When the German Blitzkrieg smashed through northern France, the British retreated to Dunkirk, but sadly there was no room for the mules on the evacuation boats...

The grooms and drivers were distressed at having to leave their animals behind in enemy territory. They gave some to local people, but most fell into German hands.

Mules were a great help to the Chindit forces in the Burmese rainforest during 1943–44. The Chindits were regular British and Commonwealth troops who fought like guerrillas. They were dropped behind Japanese lines and targeted bridges, railway lines, bases and ammunition dumps, hitting the enemy when and where they were not expecting it. The principle of the Chindits was long-range penetration and expeditions were helped enormously by thousands of mules and ponies.

In 1944, mules were dropped into the rainforest in C47 gliders, towed by Dakota transport planes. They were unimpressed by this journey and it took a lot of persuading to get them on board. One worry of fighting with mules was that they were traditionally very noisy and their braying would attract the Japanese. To prevent this, their vocal chords were painlessly severed by veterinary surgeons.

The Chindits would cover a lot of territory in the rainforest but the expedition could not have taken place without the mules carrying their machine guns, mortars, ammunition, food and water through narrow trails and sharp, rocky terrain.

Douglas Roberts was Mitzi's driver. She was a real character who wandered around the rainforest at night, but was always back

▲ Indian troops loading mule carts before sending them to the front line.

by morning. When retreating from the Japanese, the pair arrived at a dangerously fast-flowing river. Mitzi plunged in, pulling Roberts with her and, amazingly, succeeded in getting across to safety. Sadly, as he was carried off on a stretcher, exhausted, he looked back to see that Mitzi, who had saved him, had died...

A SECOND THOUGHT
Do you think it was right to sever the vocal chords of the mules that went into Burma with the Chindits?

Mountain Mules

In the summer of 1943, the Allies landed in Italy and proceeded to push north towards Rome. The German defenders were not giving up without a fight and they built the Gustav Line using the high and rocky Apennine Mountains as part of their defences. For the Allies, it was a very difficult campaign, especially in the winter. Once again, mules did their gutsy work, bringing guns and ammunition to the front line and, with special chairs, even took wounded soldiers back to the casualty stations.

▲ The Apennine mountains of Italy. Only mules could have coped with such conditions.

THE HEAVY BRIGADE

At the Animals in War Memorial in London, there are carved depictions of all the animals that have helped men in war. Two of the largest, and often the most forgotten, are the camel and the elephant. These extraordinary animals contributed to Allied successes in both World Wars...

The camel is perfectly designed for life in the harsh desert. It can carry heavy loads for long periods of time without food and water. When desert storms blow, its long protective eye-lashes and nostrils close up. Known as the 'ship of the desert', it was to be invaluable to the British in the war against the Turks in the Middle East.

In 1916, the Imperial Camel Corps was set up. Fighting the Turks meant going into rocky parts of the desert. Camels from the sandy plains of Arabia have soft pads on their feet. If they walked over flints or hot stones their soles burnt and cracked into painful blisters. Drivers had to be careful and pick gentle routes.

▼ Camels can withstand changes in body temperature and water shortages that would kill most animals.

Lawrence of Arabia

An important aspect of the war against Turkey in World War I was the Arab Revolt. Seeking freedom from the Turkish (Ottoman) Empire, Arab tribesmen attacked bases around Medina and Mecca. The British sent T.E. Lawrence (later known as 'Lawrence of Arabia') to assist the revolt. Soon, Arab attacks on railway lines, bridges and towns became legendary. Detachments of tribesmen on camels could cover vast distances, attack a target, then disappear into the desert.

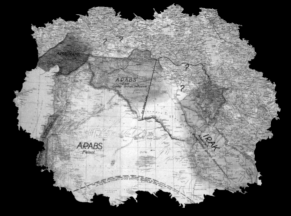

▶ Lawrence tried to assist the Arabs to gain independence. However, the Middle East was still dominated by France and Great Britain after World War I.

▲ Some elephants helped with construction work. Others were used for transport.

In World War II elephants played a key role in the British victory in Burma. When the Japanese invaded in 1942, they captured as many elephants as possible, knowing their usefulness. However, they did not treat the drivers or 'oozies' well, so at night some escaped back to British lines. The British formed the No. 1 Elephant Company led by Lieutenant Colonel James Howard Williams, who was affectionately known as 'Elephant Bill'. By 1943 they had about 60 elephants in the company. They helped to build bridges, roads and causeways through the rainforest and carried logs as though they were pencils.

In the monsoon period, when the rain fell for weeks, the elephants helped move lorries that were stuck in the mud. In March 1944, hearing of a future Japanese attack, Elephant Bill had to move the company over dangerous mountain tracks and passes to escape. The hero was Bandoola, who led the elephants over the dangerous climbs. His oozie said he knew how to close his eyes and not look down!

A SECOND THOUGHT
T.E. Lawrence and the Arab tribesmen often travelled at night. Why was this, and how did they navigate across the desert?

THE SOLDIER BEAR

In April 1942 a group of Polish soldiers who had fled from the German invasion of Russia in 1941 ('Operation Barbarossa') were a long way from home. They were in Persia (now Iran) trying to make their way to Palestine, where the 2nd Polish Corps was assembling. On the road, they noticed a half-starved boy and the men, obviously concerned, offered him some food.

▲ Wojtek as a young cub with his Polish regiment.

After a while they noticed he had a bag tied around his neck that was moving. Lance-Corporal Peter Prendys asked what was inside. It was a Syrian bear cub, bedraggled and also half-starved. The men knew the future for this bear was bleak. He would be sold as a dancing bear and experience pain and misery.

Prendys offered to buy him and money, chocolate, and a Swiss Army knife were all offered, but it was the tin of 'bully-beef' (corned beef) that swung the deal. The bear cub, now called Wojtek (meaning 'happy soldier') had joined the Polish Army! Prendys became his guardian. Although pets were not allowed in the Army, he won everyone over, even the commanding officer Major Chelminski.

The soldiers reached Iraq where there was a long delay. Wojtek suffered from the heat and was desperate for water to drink and bathe in. One day, hanging around the shower block, he slipped inside. The men heard a shriek and rushed in to find Wojtek had cornered a petrified man who turned out to be an Arab spy! Wojtek and his friends, who were now the 22nd Company, Polish Army Service Corps (Artillery), travelled through Palestine, Egypt and up through Italy. Here, they found themselves in the desperate battle of Monte Cassino, part of the attack on the German Gustav Line.

During the battle, Wojtek amazed his Company by helping to carry artillery shells for the Allied guns. One day, he picked up one of the 25-pounder shells, carried it to the storage area and went back to the lorry for some more. The men boasted that he never dropped one! The badge of the 12th Polish Regiment shows Wojtek carrying a shell. The company finally ended up in Scotland and Wojtek joined the Edinburgh Zoo. He died in 1963, aged 22.

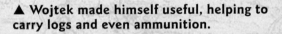
▲ Wojtek made himself useful, helping to carry logs and even ammunition.

A SECOND THOUGHT
How would Peter Prendys have felt when he had to leave Wojtek at Edinburgh Zoo after the war?

Poland

So why were Wojtek's Polish comrades dispersed, like many thousands of other Poles, all over Europe and Asia? When World War II began in August 1939, the world was shocked by the announcement of a Non-Aggression Pact between Nazi Germany and the Soviet Union. Both sides agreed not to fight each other. However, a secret clause was that if Hitler invaded Poland, both countries would split the country between them. This happened on 1 September 1939 and three weeks later Poland ceased to exist.

▲ The German invasion of Poland in September 1939.

ONE OF THE FAMILY

The men in charge of animals in wartime loved and treasured them. They liked to have animals near them and to keep them as mascots – or lucky charms – to represent their regiment, squadron or ship. When servicemen were a long way from home, families and loved ones, animals often filled the emptiness they felt.

▲ Cats are very territorial and independent, so make excellent mascots on board ship.

Ships tend to choose cats as mascots as they help keep the rat population down. HMS *Glasgow* captured a pig from a German ship during a skirmish in 1914. The Germans sunk their own ship *Dresden* to prevent it getting into enemy hands and the ship's pig swam to safety. A member of HMS *Glasgow*'s crew spotted him they hauled him aboard. Tirpitz, named after a German Admiral, became the ship's mascot until 1919.

Ordinary Sea Cat Togo was the mascot of HMS *Irresistible* between 1904 and 1915. Togo died when the ship was sunk during the Dardanelles Campaign in 1915. In World War II some famous Royal Navy ships adopted cats as mascots. HMS *Duke of York* had Whiskey and HMS *Belfast* had a tiny little kitten called Frankenstein. When both ships took part in the Battle of the North Cape on Boxing Day 1943, Whiskey slept soundly during the roar of the 14-inch guns! Russian sailors at Murmansk had previously given *Belfast* a reindeer, Rudolf, as a mascot, but she died of fright during the battle.

Army regiments have traditionally adopted goats as mascots. This started during the Crimean War (1853–56) with Taffy, who was beautifully groomed and belonged to

Mascot Morale

Mascots had a very positive effect on the morale of servicemen in war. Many commanders noticed that men became more positive when there was an animal in their company. During war, men rarely got leave and they were short of affection in their lives. When Minnie – the pony born into war-torn Burma – was badly injured, Commander 'Mad' Mike Calvert insisted that news about her condition be sent to all fighting units. They were overjoyed when she survived…

▲ Hoping for some morsels, the ship's cat joins the sailors on the mess deck table!

the 2nd Battalion Welsh Regiment. The regimental goat, Taffy IV, actually saw service in Word War I taking part in the famous retreat from Mons and the first Battle of Ypres, October–November 1914. Taffy died on 20 January 1915, but was awarded the famous campaign medal, the 1914 Star.

A SECOND THOUGHT

Do you think taking animals to war as mascots was a good or bad thing?

▼ Taffy, the regimental goat, with soldiers of the 16th Service Battalion. They went to France in 1915.

RESEARCH AND RECORDS

Y ou have learned about the exceptional contribution that animals made to the two World Wars. Contributions that, for a long time, were unrecognised. So, are these stories true and what are they based on? How do we know Taffy served with the 2nd Battalion Welsh Regiment? Where is the evidence that Rob, the para-dog, made 20 jumps into war zones? Is there documentary proof that G.I. Joe saved the lives of so many soldiers?

Where do historians get their information from? It is a lot more complicated than studying old books. Our knowledge of the past comes from evidence that has been left behind. A lot of this evidence is written on paper, but paper can get lost or destroyed. To keep this evidence safe, it is stored in places called archives. If a historian was researching how pigeons were used in the war they would visit an archive that held papers, letters, drawings, photographs and documents. The National Archives at Kew in London, is one of the biggest Britain.

◀ **Document showing instructions for the release of carrier pigeons.**

▶ A late13th-century drawing of mounted warrior with spear.

The National Archives is the most important archive in Britain and specialises in documents that are connected with the governing of the country. At Kew, you can view and touch official papers that date back to the 11th century. The vast majority relate to the 19th to 21st centuries but documents from the middle ages to the early modern (16th century) period are carefully preserved. You can even find out how much Henry VIII spent on his horses when he met the French King, Francis I, near Calais, in 1520!

◀ Some documents at the archive are incredibly fragile and have to be handled with great care.

GLOSSARY

Artillery – Large guns that fire heavy exploding shells.

Ballistic missile – A long range weapon that reaches its target by free falling at very high speeds on a specific place.

Blitz – The bombing of British towns and cities during 1940–45.

Blitzkrieg – A German word for an intense attack, meaning 'lightning war'.

Chindits – British and Commonwealth troops fighting behind Japanese lines in Burma 1943–44.

Conscription – Called up to do compulsory military service.

Gallantry – Showing great courage in the face of danger.

Gestapo – The secret police force of Nazi Germany.

Guerrilla – Fighters who make sudden attacks on a bigger force or army behind enemy lines. From the Spanish meaning 'little war'.

Imperial Camel Corps – A British and Commonwealth camel-mounted infantry brigade used in the Middle East, 1916–19.

Liberate – To free from the control of another country.

Limber – Part of a gun carriage that often carried ammunition.

Loft – A place or building that homing pigeons are kept in and return to.

Luftwaffe – The air force of Nazi Germany.

Mascot – An animal that brings good luck to a group or organisation.

Mine – An explosive device, often hidden and detonated by pressure.

Mule – A cross between a horse and a donkey.

Oozie – The local Burmese name for an elephant 'driver'.

PDSA – People's Dispensary for Sick Animals.

PDSA Dickin Medal – A medal awarded to animals for gallantry in military service. It has been awarded since 1943.

Royal Army Veterinary Corps – A branch of the British Army that trains and looks after animals.

RSPCA – Royal Society for the Prevention of Cruelty to Animals.

Shell shock – A condition of intense fear brought on by traumatic experiences in war or conflict.

Shrapnel – Balls of lead that are released from an exploding shell.

Sniffer dog – A specialist dog used for its strong sense of smell.

V1 – A jet-propelled bomb used by Nazi Germany.

V2 – A rocket carrying high explosives launched by Nazi Germany. It was the first missile to leave the earth's atmosphere.

Veteran – A person or animal who has long experience of a particular activity.

FURTHER INFORMATION

BOOKS

Animals at War: In Association with the Imperial War Museum by Isobel George and Rob Lloyd James, Usborne Publishing (2006)

Animals in War (Collins Big Cat Progress) by Jillian Powell, Collins Educational (2012)

Bonzo's War: Animals under Fire 1939–45 by Clare Campbell, Constable (2013)

The Animals' War: Animals in Wartime from the First World War to the Present Day by Juliet Gardner, Portrait (2006)

The Bomber Dog by Megan Rix, Puffin (2013)

War Dog (EDGE – A Rivets Short Story) by Chris Ryan, Franklin Watts (2013)

WEBSITES

www.nationalarchives.gov.uk
Website of The National Archives. Follow education links for pages on the World Wars.

www.ams-museum.org.uk/museum/ravc-history/
Army Medical Services website, with a good section on Royal Army Veterinary Corps.

www.pdsa.org.uk/about-us/animal-bravery-awards
Website of the People's Dispensary for Sick Animals – with a section on Dickin Medal winners.

www.historylearningsite.co.uk/animals_in_world_war_one.htm
Excellent information on horses, dogs and pigeons in World War I.

INDEX